It is still illegal to grow marijuana in most states and countries. Therefore, the author and publisher recommend you read this book for your own information and enjoyment.

How to Grow the Finest Marijuana Indoors Under Lights

Compiled By
Joseph Carver

Fertilizer & Hydroponics by
Muggles MacGregor
Illustrations by Evelyn Schmevelyn
&
Newt Foster

Published by Homestead Book Company
PO Box 31608
Seattle Wa 98103

Wholesale / Retail Inquiries
Homestead Book Company
1-800-426-6777

ISBN 0-930180-14-3

Table of Contents

This book discusses the use of metal halide and sodium vapor lights, which make it possible for you to grow the finest marijuana in your home.

Using these lights you can create an environment very much like that of Hawaii. You will find that the taste and potency of plants grown in this environment will likely surpass anything you have previously grown.

This book was first written in 1978. A few techniques have changed. Some photos are outdated but the text has been completely updated. It is still just as easy to grow a small garden of marijuana for your own use. Keep in mind that the U.S. government is actively prosecuting people growing their own marijuana, consequently, discretion is of utmost importance.

In Canada, there appears to be a much more enlightened view on the subject.

Growing indoors enables you to control the environment, and to keep "pests" away from your plants.

Chapter 1
Choosing Your Seeds or Cuttings

1. ... na... gv
low ... wer, e... ...ilk...
2. ... pie... of gol... ...ne...
mar'i-graph. ... [... m ... the ...ea ...nd
ein, to w... ... n ...utomatic ...
measuring ... king ... continu...
the height of the tide
mä-rĭ-juä'nä, mä-rĭ-huä'nä (-hwä')
hemp plant, *Cannabis sativa*, or its
and flowers, toxic when smoked in
mar-i-kĭ'... ... ... m native nan
ol... y, ...h Americ... ...m
fin... silk... ha... ... golden-ye...
man... ... ...e neck; also calle
tam...
... ...n. [Port.] A musical
... ...rs o... different lengths
... ...en struck; a ki
... da, ...n. [Sp.] A spide
... ...h) of Central and Sou
... ...d'), n. [Fr.] pickle,
... ...ro... L. *mare*, the sea.] .

Marijuana seeds

This seedling was planted seven days ago

A newly sprouted seed with the shell still attached

8

This female cutting is about 12 days old

Most growers start their plants from female cuttings for two reasons: a female plant is guaranteed and harvest time comes sooner than starting a crop from seed. Female cuttings are essential because they are the bud-producing plants. If you are unable to get female cuttings, you will have to start from seed. The seeds will need to be grown and flowered to determine whether they are male or female plants. See chapter 8 (pg.72) for determining the sex of your plants.

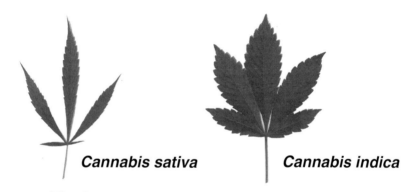

Cannabis sativa | ***Cannabis indica***

The best marijuana you can grow will come from the seeds or cuttings of the highest quality marijuana you can obtain. Strains of Cannabis Indica are the best varieties for indoor growing because they take less time to mature and do not grow too tall (about 5'). Indica, native to Afghanistan and the Hindu Kush, has large leaves with resinous colas (flower tops) and is grown for the production of hashish (processed resin).

The plants from Southeast Asia (Thailand and Vietnam) are some of the most potent in the world. They take longer to bloom than those from Afghanistan and grow twice as tall. Most marijuana from Hawaii probably originated in Southeast Asia and was brought to the islands by the trading traffic.

For thousands of years, marijuana has been a cultivated plant. Perhaps it was one of the first plants to be actively grown and tended. Few plants offer such a diversity of products to the cultivator; strong fiber (hemp), nutritious seeds, oil, and resin which has an interesting effect on the central nervous system. It is impossible to say for which of its properties the plant was first grown, but it is certain that all were quickly exploited. Each country, tribe and village soon had its own distinct strain, with characteristics reflecting the climate, cultivation techniques and ultimate desires of the cultivators. Some plants were grown for the fiber and seed oil (these plants are worthless as resin producers), while others were selected for high THC (tetrahydrocannabinol) content and were used much as the same types of marijuana today. The strains that make good rope do not produce the most potent flowering tops.

10

Marijuana is a domesticated plant in the sense that it can be grown successfully yet retain the ability to survive and flourish in the wild. There is no way of knowing without extensive study (and federal funding), exactly how many distinct strains of marijuana there are or what properties they possess.

The most logical thing to do is pick the seeds out of the best pot you can find and use them for your first crop. There are benefits to learning the origin of the seeds, as you might use the information in later breeding projects for new generations. A breeding program may be as simple as choosing the seeds from the best plant in the first crop and using them for the second, or it can become a major project if you have the space available for it.

Most people use female cuttings rather than starting from seeds. A harvest from cuttings takes two to four months to mature, versus three to seven months from seed. If you don't know any growers with spare genetic material, you will have to plant seeds. As they grow, identify each plant with a different name or color. Take cuttings from each plant, identifying it with the parent plant. Cut back the light to the parent plants to allow the plants to flower. Eliminate the males and the corresponding male cuttings. You now have your own strain of female, bud producing, seed free marijuana (Sinsemilla).

Your plants must have a dark period to bloom

11

Seeds generally will germinate immediately after they are mature on the plant. Some of the less domesticated strains may require a period of dormancy, or even cold treatment. Seeds are mature when the seed pod splits open and the seeds turn dark.

Germination of seeds takes anywhere from 12 hours to a week, although most seeds will sprout in a few days. Take the seeds and place them about 1/8 to 1/4 inch below the surface of the growing medium. This medium could be soil, or better yet, a rockwool cube. Rockwool can be found at many garden supply stores. Rockwool is an insulation-like medium that is clean, very effective and easy to use. The main advantages to using this product is when you moisten it and place your seeds or cuttings in the hole on top, there is no need to ever disturb the roots again. When the roots appear, all you have to do is place the cube into a four or six inch pot with soil. The rooting medium should be kept warm (70 - 75 degrees), located under fluorescent or low wattage halide lights. The roots must never dry out. Do not allow your rockwool to remain in standing water.

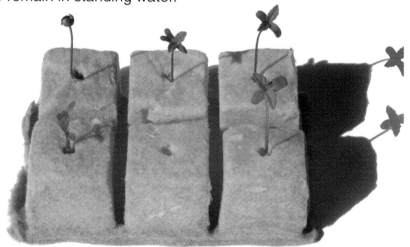

Seedlings in rockwool cubes

12

Rockwool is a great medium for starting seeds or cuttings

Color coded labels are used to identify different strains.

Seeds are ripe as soon as the seed pod splits open

13

Step one

Step two

Step three

14

These roots look very healthy. While this plant could be transplanted into a two gallon pot and flowered right now, a longer period of vegetative growth would increase the ultimate yield.

Chapter 2

Lighting

The main problem in growing outstanding marijuana indoors is providing enough light. With the metal halide lamp, it is hard to fail. Even with average seeds and average soil, you'll get excellent results using halides, adequate water and proper nutrients.

The high pressure sodium lamp has a distinct amber color

Fluorescent lights   The first light to install is a fluorescent light for growing seeds, cuttings and plants. Although you will need a halide light at some point, the fluorescent lights play an even more important role in your continuous quest for a personal supply. You will need a two or four light fixture. If you use two tubes, be sure the fixture has a reflector shield. You might also use four tubes lined up. This will increase germination rate, growth, rooting and area coverage.

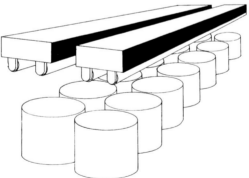

Fluorescent lamps If you can find any of the following bulbs, use them. Verilux, Vita Lite, Standard Gro Lux, or Lumichrome 5000. Or you could also try Sylvania D-50, Philips Chroma-50, Philips Agro, or a Daylight. The better bulbs are worth the cost. Don't settle for less. Better bulbs offer quality parts, longer life, extended warranties and better color spectrums.

H.I.D. or High intensity discharge lights which include mercury vapor, metal halide and high pressure sodium, have been used for many years in many capacities. Street lighting, commercial, and industrial lighting are examples of the uses of mercury vapor and sodium vapor (orange street lights). The type that we will be dealing with in the book are the **metal halide** and the **high pressure sodium.** There are several wattages available; the most commonly used sizes are the 250, 400, and 1000 watt units.

Metal Halide lamp

Complete unit. This includes the ballast, wired to the reflector and lamp.

Inside the ballast box there are two or three components. The *transformer* is the largest and heaviest part.

The *capacitor* is the can-like unit that has two wires coming off the top.

The *starter* or *ignitor* is only found in high pressure sodiums.

High pressure sodium lamp

Halide vs. Sodium Both halide and sodium lamps are very effective at growing and flowering marijuana. It has been disputed as to which is the ideal light source, and each has advantages. Halides contain all the colors in the spectrum, are less expensive than high pressure sodium bulbs (HPS), and burn at their best for one year. HPS bulbs have more of the red spectrum which plants need during the flowering stage, but do not have as much blue light, which is necessary for compact growth. HPS bulbs need replacement every other year. Because halides have the full color spectrum, they make an excellent choice for the indoor gardener.

An exception to the halide recommendation is the 430 Son Agro sodium which was developed for horticultural use. This HPS bulb made by Philips has more blue light to make it an excellent all around light source.

Clear or Phosphorous Halide bulb?

Either bulb will do, but we recommend that you get a coated one rather than a clear one. Clear lamps have a higher light output, more blue light, and cost a few dollars less but the higher light output means little since light level measurements are based on the human eye, and plants respond to a different range of colors. A coated lamp is suggested because they have more red light and are easier on the eyes.

One other note about halide bulbs. There are metal halide bulbs (MH), and metal super bulbs (MS). The MS bulb has a higher output, as much as 25% more. These lamps will have a specific burning position, i.e. horizontal or vertical depending on the lamp.

How much light? Use approximately 25 watts per square foot of floor space.

Let's say your area has a floor space of 4 feet by 5 feet.

4' x 5' = 20 square feet. 20 sq. ft **x** 25 watts = 500 watts. A 400 watt halide will do fine, as long as reflectivity is optimized.

This room has mylar on the walls to increase the light

This is a comparison of light output in *Lumens*, which is a measurement of light based on what the human eye sees. Plants see different light than the human eye.

1000 watt super metal halide (MS1000)	125,000
1000 watt standard halide (MH1000)	100,000
400 watt super metal halide (MS 400)	40,000
250 watt super metal halide (MS250HOR)	23,000
1000 watt high pressure sodium	140,000
430 watt Son Agro	53,000
400 watt high pressure sodium	47,000
250 watt high pressure sodium	28,500
1000 watt mercury vapor lamp	47,000
100 watt incandescent (light bulb)	1,000

There is very little ultra violet light emitted from halide or sodium bulbs

22

A by-product of the light is heat. Your light source will be an adequate source of heat in the creation of the perfect environment for your plant. If you have ever tried indoor marijuana cultivation with anything other than an HID light you have learned that warm temperatures with inadequate light produces spindly plants. When you combine a warm environment with an abundance of light, the heat will act with the light to produce a growing environment similar to outdoors.

Now, more than ever, people are growing for their own personal and medical use. Smaller gardens are great for people who would like to grow enough for their personal stash without spending money every month. If you are concerned about using outrageous amounts of power, a 400 watt light only uses about $10.00 per month in electricity.

The average life expectancy of halide bulbs is 10,000 hours, or about two years at 12 hours per day, although they often burn longer. You should replace your lamp at least once a year. This is important because bulbs lose as much as 40% of their original output after one year of use.

One 1000 watt halide light could provide enough light for 25 plants or more in 10 inch containers in an area 7' x 7'. Each plant may produce as much as 1/4 to 1/2 ounce of bud per plant. More is possible with good genetics and growth techniques, but don't count your buds until they are cured.

Feel free to walk on the grass

23

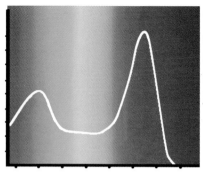

The plant photosynthesis curve. Contrary to the human eye, plants see the blue and red light more than green and yellow.

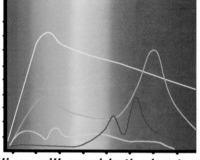

Yellow - Sunlight
Green - Plant Photosynthesis
Blue - Metal Halide lamp
Purple - High Pressure
Sodium

Here you can see that a combination of halide and sodium will provide the best color spectrum for plant photo synthesis, halide offering the blue, and sodium the far red.

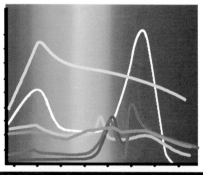

The 430 watt Son Agro HPS bulb has more blue light- enough blue to keep plant growth compact. Either an Agro sodium or a metal halide will help produce great plants.

Yellow - Sunlight
White - Plant Photosynthesis
Lt Blue -ClearHalide lamp
Dk Blue - Coated Halide lamp
Purple -Son Agro
Red - HPS

Plants that are grown outside may be exposed to over 10,000 footcandles, (a measurement of light, equivalent to one candle at one foot).

A 1000 watt halide provides 2500 footcandles at 16 inches.

Although the levels of light indoors are much less than outdoors, in most circumstances plants grown indoors seem to adapt and grow as well or better than those grown outside, because other factors affecting growth can be optimized.

Sodium for Flowering? If you would like to improve your flowering potential, you should consider using a sodium conversion bulb in your halide unit. This is a sodium bulb that will operate in your metal halide system.

The conversion bulb will cost about $200 for a 1000 watt, or $100 for a 400 or 250 watt.

This amber colored light is heavy in the red spectrum, which plants need during the flowering cycle.

Halide lights satisfy almost all the requirements of a perfect indoor light source. The cost of operation is minimal. 1000 watts is equal to one kilowatt. The price per kilowatt hour, meaning the price of using 1000 watts of electricity for one hour, varies from area to area.

At five cents per kilowatt hour, a 1000 watt light will cost five cents per hour to run. At 18 hours a day for a month it will cost $27.00. At 12 hours a day for a month, it will cost $18.00. You can find out how much you are charged per kilowatt hour by looking at your electric bill.

Where do I get these lights? These lights can be purchased through a large number of lighting or electrical stores, or from a greenhouse supplier. Make sure you shop at a reputable dealer, be careful what you say, and don't ask stupid questions. You might get asked to leave the store, and if things are not going your way, you might possibly get a visit by an agent from the local DEA. Be cautious purchasing halide lights from any company that has opened since the 1989 Green Merchant raids. There are some retailers and mail order companies that may be DEA sting operations.

Reflective Surfaces

Take advantage of your walls. A reflective surface will reflect light back at the plants. The increase is dramatic and this practice is highly recommended. Mylar is easy to apply, and is faster and cleaner than paint. This is an excellent option when painting isn't. Paint will provide longer lasting results because the mylar gets dirty, especially when using foliar sprays.

Reflective percentages

Mylar	91 %
Flat white paint	86%
Sheet rock	80%
White plastic	82%
Mirror	75%

Reflectors There are many hoods or reflectors to choose from. Choose the reflector that best suits the shape and size of the room. White walls and ceilings in smaller areas may not require a shield. Keep in mind that large reflectors trap large amounts of heat.

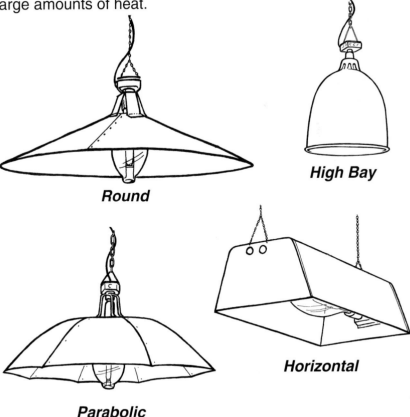

Round

High Bay

Parabolic

Horizontal

27

These plants are being grown under metal halide. They have not been exposed to any darkness

You can grow your cuttings for a month or two under fluorescent lights with 24 hours of day-length. When you feel the plants are reaching the size you desire, take cuttings, and move the plants under the HID light that is on a 12 hour on/ off cycle.

Marijuana is a "tender perennial" grown as an annual. This means that it can be regenerated indoors. In tropical climates marijuana can survive for several years.

An annual grows during the spring and summer, and flowers in the fall.

It is the short days that make marijuana flower. Cuttings and seedlings should be grown under 24 hours of light so that they remain in the growing state for about two months. After two months, change the light to a 12 hour day, and a 12 hour night. This short day will cause the plant to bloom.

Chapter 3
Setting up the growing area

One 1000 watt metal halide light will effectively provide light for an area of at least six by six feet. If you paint the room bright white or use mylar as a reflector, you can increase this area to eight by eight. There is obviously no limit as to how large or small the room can be, but it must have at least enough space to hang the lights and still have enough room to move about and care for the plants. The smaller the room you use and the more lights, the greater the amount of excess heat produced. A properly designed exhaust system will help to eliminate these heat problems.

A circulation fan

Lack of ventilation is a common problem for the indoor grower. It is important to make sure that the air is freely moving over the plants. Respiration cannot occur properly if the air is stagnant. If the air is not relatively fresh, the plant will grow slower, and often succumb to pests, disease and respiratory ailments that normally would not affect it.

The more plants in a room, the more important it is that fresh air is introduced. The plants use carbon dioxide and once this gas is depleted, the growth rate slows down.

In addition, the room gains humidity as the water evaporates from the soil. The plant itself gives off H_2O when it breathes. This is known as evapo-transpiration. It is better for the plants if you can maintain medium humidity in the area. By forcing the stale air out of the room, you draw in fresh air that is higher in CO_2 content and is usually less humid.

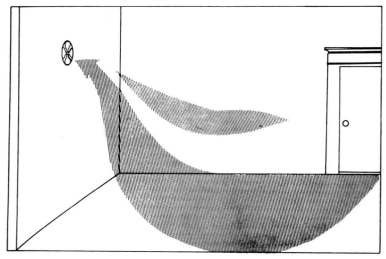

You can easily install a negative-pressure ventilation system by making a hole in one side of the room above plant height, into which you fit the fan. Face the fan outwards in order to exhaust the air from the room. This will pull new fresh air into the growing area. The fan can be regulated by a thermostat and or humidistat so that it only comes on when the temperature or humidity reaches a certain level.

Temperature of the air

Once you have established your growing system and have provided yourself with as many of the positive controls available to you. You will want to know about how to control these factors to the plant's best advantage. During the hours that the light is on, the ideal air temperature is between 75 and 85 degrees. This temperature can vary a little with no apparent effect, but generally speaking, if you are using a strong enough light source, a warmer temperature is beneficial to growth and probably to resin production as well. It is best for the plants if the temperature stays below 90 degrees. At night the plant's functions change, and a cooler temperature, in the 65° to 75° degree range is recommended.

The squirrel cage blower is the most effective exhaust fan.

Air Temperature

High - 85°   Low - 65°

Timers

A timer will allow you to control the number of hours your light is on and off. Plugging and unplugging it is not a reasonable replacement for a timer.

Using the correct timer for your light is important. Make sure that the timer is properly rated for the amp draw of your light. Timers will list three different amp ratings, so you need to note the "inductive" rating.

A 1000 watt halide draws 9.5 amps when running at 120 volts. A 400 watt halide draws 4.7 amps at 120volts. Most timers will be adequate for 400 watts, but many fall short of the 1000 watt inductive rating.

Be sure that your timer is properly grounded with a three prong connector.

The heavy duty timers are recommended. These timers are rated for 40 amps which will be more than adequate. These timers may cost $60 for the timer only, or up to $120 for one that is wired.

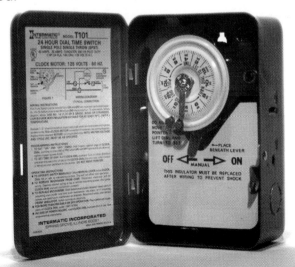

A 40 Amp timer

Electricity

When you plan on setting up your growing area, you need to make sure that you have enough power available.

Your HID light is the main consumer of power in your room. The exhaust fan, fluorescent lights, and circulation fans will also need to be considered.

Most of the circuit breakers in your home will be 15 or 20 amps. This number will be on the switch itself. A 20 amp breaker can accommodate a 1000 watt light as well as a blower and fluorescent light with no problem. A 15 amp breaker may not handle that load.

For smaller gardens with 250 or 400 watt lights, you will never trip a breaker unless you run a vacuum or hair dryer on the same circuit. These small gardens use a minimal amount of electricity, and energy consumption will hardly be noticed on the power bill.

240 Volts

There are three common appliances that will use 240 volts: the hot water heater, the stove, and the dryer. The hot water tank is usually wired direct, and you are not likely to be growing in your kitchen. The dryer has a 240 volt plug, and this is often a good source of power.

Using 240 volts does not reduce your electricity consumption, but it does allow you to use fewer amps. Lights use half the amps on 240 volts compared to 120 volts. This means you can run two 1000 watt lights and only be drawing 9.5 amps.

240 volt timers can be wired with a dryer cord so your lights can all be on the same cycle. You can also split the 240 into 120's (shown in photo). This is often easier since most fans run on 120 volts.

You can increase your lighting coverage with the use of a light mover. Track devices will cost between $100 and $200. They move the reflector and lamp and this spreads out the light, eliminating the effects of shading. It is best to get a track that pauses at the end in order for the light to be distributed evenly. There are also circular light movers that work with one, two, or three lights.

As discussed in the lighting chapter, using mylar or flat white paint will ensure the even distribution of light to the plants. If using white paint, apply it before starting your garden, as paint fumes can be toxic to plants.

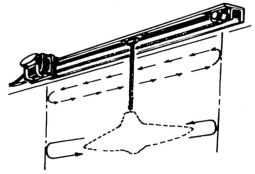

A light track moves the light back and forth

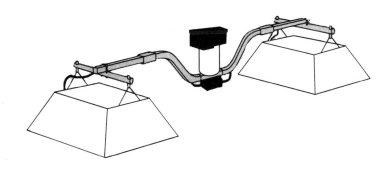

A "Sun Circle" revolves 360 degrees. They come in one, two, or three light systems

Filtering the odors

Charcoal filters have been the most popular and affordable means of removing odors from your growing area. Second only to other growers (turned government informants), odor is the main reason people get busted.

Passing air through one or two layers of charcoal will decrease the odors. The odor is absorbed by the charcoal. Activated charcoal is more effective, but it is more expensive than horticultural grade. Replace horticultural charcoal after every harvest.

Designs of the filter will vary depending on your space. Purchasing a unit for a large area could be costly, so designing your own is recommended.

Many filters are available at local department stores. These filters will often use charcoal or negative ion technology.

A round filter is the most efficient because there is more surface area of charcoal to absorb the odors

Ozone generator

An ozone gererator is the most effective means of odor control. This small generator will produce O_3. O_3 is an unstable form of oxygen known as ozone which will remove the odor from the air. This unit can be built into your exhaust chamber and will mix with the air on its way out. This generator is extremely effective but costly, as well as difficult to find. A unit may cost anywhere from $400 to $900. They are commonly used to remove smoke odors from a house which has burned and to remove bacteria from hospital air.

Ozone is mixed with the exhaust from the grow room to help eliminate the odor produced by growing marijuana. Because ozone can be toxic to plants and animals it is highly recommended that the ozone be mixed with the exhaust as shown in the diagram below.

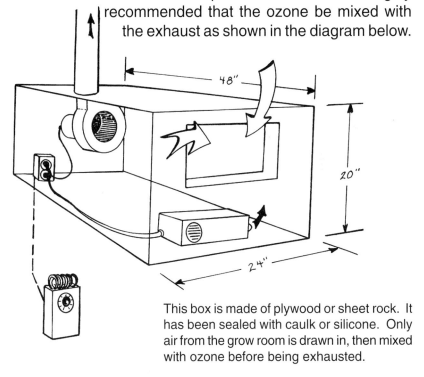

This box is made of plywood or sheet rock. It has been sealed with caulk or silicone. Only air from the grow room is drawn in, then mixed with ozone before being exhausted.

Important: Ozone generator and exhaust blower are switched on and off by the thermostat inside the growing area.

How to build a charcoal filter

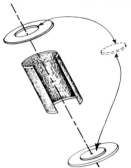

A frame is cut out of wood, and the center screen is applied.

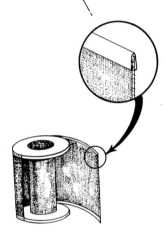

Both the inside and outside of the cylinder should be two layers of screen. Use window screen to hold the charcoal in, and a larger, stronger screen to give the filter strength. Hold these together with duct tape.

Exhaust fan

A hole for filling the filter with charcoal

Once you have your unit complete, a fan will pull the air through the charcoal and the odors will be reduced.

CO$_2$ Enrichment

If the area can be made relatively air tight, carbon dioxide gas may be introduced. This practice is helpful, although it may be unnecessary, or more trouble than it's worth. CO$_2$ enrichment must be done while the lights are on and the fans are off. This poses a problem with temperature build-up. To set up a CO$_2$ system it will often cost upwards of $500, while a good ventilation system will cost only a couple hundred dollars.

The use of CO$_2$ could be beneficial, but is often more trouble than it's worth

"There is a lot of CO_2 to breathe but it sure is hot!"

Chapter 4 Soil

The best soil you can find is the only soil you should buy

The soil you choose for your plants is a primary factor in determining their ultimate growth and health. The texture of the soil is the most important feature and soil quality should be given first priority along with environmental control (lighting and temperature). Soil should be loose and crumbly, and should fall apart in your hands as you squeeze it. A loose, porous soil lets air circulate freely and allows even drying. It should absorb water easily. A dense, tightly packed soil mixture will constrict the roots and prevent their normal rate of growth. The soil functions in the plant system similar to how the stomach and lungs function in the body. Food absorption and gas exchange take place in the soil. Heavy soil that cakes on top and dries hard will inhibit the exchange of gas, stunt the root growth, slow the foliage growth, and inhibit the effectiveness of fertilizer.

Excellent plants can be grown in both organic and inorganic soil. You can achieve basically the same results using organic and inorganic fertilizers. The choice is strictly up to you as to whether or not to try for an organic system. Plants grown with organic fertilizer and soil may have a better taste when smoked.

Soil from the garden is the cheapest, but it is also the most likely to contain spider mites, bad thrips and all sorts of nasty pathogens. Do not use garden soil.

Artificial, or soilless, mixes have the advantage of sterility and uniformity. You can mix up batches of soilless mixtures and they will be the same every time.

The most common component of a well made soilless mix is peat moss; this is always used with a drainage aid such as pumice, perlite, or vermiculite. These will not only create an evenly draining mix, they will also help supply the roots with oxygen. Although peat moss is organic, it has very little nutrient value.

Some of these ingredients are technically inorganic materials, but a better word would be inert. They will not interfere with organic processes. In addition to these other ingredients, there will be lime, wetting agent, and some nutrients added to make the potting mix complete. Lime will help maintain a neutral pH in the medium, since peat moss is acidic. Wetting agents help the peat take on water instead of repelling the water.

Making your own soil is a lot of work and it is usually not recommended. If you cannot find a soil that you like, you can supplement a packaged soil with one of many additives such as worm castings, bat guano, or pumice to improve drainage.

Don't buy soil that has lots of wood chips or sawdust. Wood will decompose and turn the soil acidic. If the soil is too acidic, the plant cannot assimilate nitrogen, resulting in the leaves turning yellow.

The natural fertilizer in organic soil may or may not be enough to provide the plant with food throughout its entire life cycle. You may have to supplement the plant's diet near the end of the cycle, should the soil become depleted. You can use a dilute organic fertilizer in frequent supplementary feedings.

Worm castings A very good additive for soil is worm castings, a by-product of worm farms. The worms take in organic matter, which passes through their bodies and is deposited in the soil and then sold as castings for fertilizer. A gallon costs about $4.95 and should supplement four to ten gallons of soil.

Whether you use organic or artificial mixes, the pH should be between 6.4 and 7.0. You can buy commercial mixes which are the correct pH or you can buy a pH test kit. If the soil is acidic, the pH is below seven. If the pH is above seven, the soil is alkaline. To raise the pH of the soil, add lime, or better yet, "pH Up", a product which raises the alkaline level of soil or fertilizer solution.

If your mix is a peat moss medium you may have to add some "pH Up" since the peat is quite acidic, (around 4.5.) Do not add any lime or "pH Up" until you have confirmed that the pH is in fact below 6.0. Many quality soil blends will already have lime added and an additional raise in the pH may be harmful. (See page 55 for more detailed information on pH levels.)

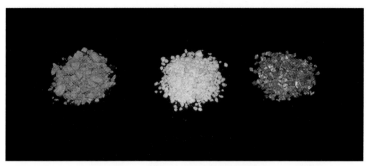

Pumice, perlite, and vermiculite. Common aeration supplements for a peat based soil mix.

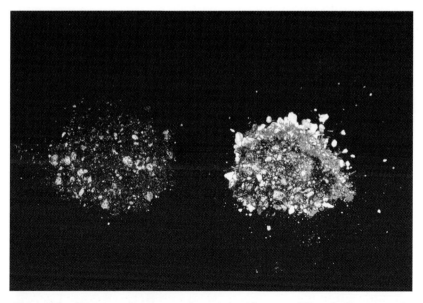

Two similar peat moss based mixes. The left sample contains worm castings, and both have pumice.

Transplanting

Remove the plant from the small pot by flexing the plastic and turning the plant over. Do not pull hard on the stem.

This is the proper way to hold the plant until you set it into the soil.

Prepare your next container by placing some soil on the bottom. Place the plant onto the new soil. Be sure that the surface level of the old soil will still be at the top of the new soil surface. Do not bury any of the stem.

Then fill up the sides with soil and lightly pack it. Water the soil with a mild nutrient, as well as a vitamin supplement.

Chapter 5
Containers

One type of container that seems to work quite well is a grow bag available at plant stores. These heavy duty plastic bags are very compact and inexpensive. Simply fill the bag with soil like you would a normal container.

Plastic nursery cans are the easiest to work with.

The fiber pot is a compressed peat pot. These containers are earth friendly.

These four-week-old indica cuttings were transplanted into a one gallon pot

The same plants as above, six weeks later

The rooted cutting in rockwool can be potted directly into soil

Chapter 6
Watering

Whenever you water your plants, water them thoroughly. You should make sure that the pots are draining properly. If a little water comes out the bottom when you water, it is a good sign. If you do not get the soil completely wet when you water, dry pockets will result. Any roots caught in a dry pocket will be damaged, perhaps permanently. The water will also leach excess salts out of the soil. The build-up of fertilizer salts in the soil will cause alkalinity and the flushing of these salts is a good idea.

When to water is a question only answered by the plant itself. You don't have to wait until the plant says that it is dying before you water. However, ideally, you want to provide the roots with the best conditions in which to do their work at optimum level. The root system picks up water and oxygen, products of metabolism. If the soil is kept too wet, all the oxygen is forced away from the roots and they suffocate. If the soil dries out too much for too long, the delicate hair roots wither and lose their ability to provide the plant with oxygen, water and nutrients from the soil. The roots love small humid air pockets between moist soil particles.

Moisture meters, obtained in most plant shops, work well when checking the moisture level six or eight inches deep. This is important with larger pots.

The best moisture meter is your pointer finger. Scoop the top half inch of soil with one finger to see and feel the moisture level just below the surface. Once the soil is dry at this point, it is time to water.

You have at least three clues when to water; the size of the pot, the size of the plant, and the moisture level in the top layer of soil. Small plants in small pots, such as seedlings or cuttings in one to four inch pots should be watered as soon as the surface is dry. The larger the plant gets, the faster the soil will dry out and the more often you will have to water. You should try and avoid growing large plants in pots that are too small, but if they do get away from you, remember that the larger the plant, the more water it uses. The smaller the plant the less water it uses, so that a small plant in a large pot must be watered less often. As the plant grows, it will progressively consume more water and fertilizer at a faster rate.

Field of dreams?
If you plant it, it will grow!

Saucers will keep your area clean and dry, as well as aid in watering the plants. Make sure your saucer is not too small, otherwise it will overflow every time you water. Allow the water to drain into the saucer. The plants can soak for about five minutes while the soil sponges up the water. If this happens you can be sure that there was a dry pocket in the soil, and it was a good idea to leave the water. If after five minutes the water is still standing, you should empty the water from the saucer. It is best to purchase the heavy duty green or white plastic saucers instead of the clear plastic. The clear ones break down very quickly.

If the soil becomes very dried out you can submerge the pot into another container full of water, and soak the soil for about half a minute.

If the soil should dry out too far, it may be hard for you to remoisten it. The surface tension of the hardened soil may resist the water and many times extremely dry soil will pull away from the sides of the pot. To soften very dry soil, you can water repeatedly, waiting a few minutes between watering or you can water from the bottom. A wetting agent may be necessary.

The water from the tap varies from place to place. The amount of chemicals such as chlorine in your tap water varies from area to area. Chlorine is a poison and can stunt your plants. This can be minimized by filling containers of water a day prior to watering. Chlorine is dissipated when it is exposed to light. In addition, the water will have a chance to warm up to room temperature, this will eliminate cold water shock.

Rain water is sometimes a good source of clean water. However, in the city, rain water often mixes with the industrial waste in the air and has large amounts of sulfuric acid in it. Also be careful when collecting water from the roof drainage because it might pick up toxic chemicals from the surface of the roof.

You can test the water by sending a sample and some money to a laboratory. Look in the yellow pages under "Laboratories."

Store containers of water for 24 hours to dissipate the chlorine and raise the temperature to room level.

pH

Litmus Paper
pH test kit

The pH is a scale, measuring the acidity or alkalinity of something. The pH level of the soil, water, or nutrient solution is important for the health of the plant.

The scale is from 1-15, 1 being acid, 15- alkaline.

Seven is neutral. Six is ten times more acidic than seven, and five is one hundred times more acidic than seven, and so on.

Keep the soil pH between 6 and 7. There are soil test kits and there are water test kits. Testing the water is important because this effects the pH of the soil.

Test your water straight from the tap, and again after you add your nutrient solution.

Litmus paper test. The proper method is to place water and a piece of litmus paper into the test tube, wait one minute, and match match a color. To measure soil pH, mix two parts by volume of distilled water to one part soil, shake and let settle for fifteen minutes, then strain (if necessary) and measure the pH of the resulting solution.

Liquid test kits are also very easy to use. Put a few drops in the test tube and match the color.

Digital meters are the most accurate and easy to read. They start at $80 and go up to $300. Use a calibration solution to keep the meter accurate, make sure you rinse the probes after each use, and store it properly.

Inexpensive soil probes may be helpful at best, but they are difficult to read since the meter jumps all over the place. They will give you a general idea if you are not sure where the pH stands.

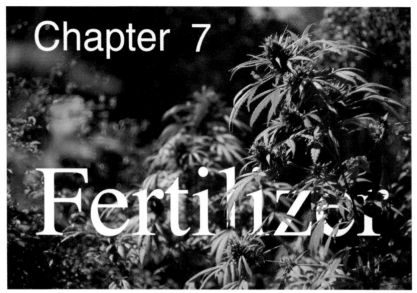

Chapter 7
Fertilizer

By Muggles MacGregor

Put simply, the difference between so-called "organic" and hydroponic or mineral-salt based fertilizers is whether the soil or the plant is being fed. "Organic" is more of a bureaucratic definition of what materials and procedures are allowable for the certification of produce, than it is a coherent philosophy. Of course, it makes sense to build healthy soil if one's garden is in the great outdoors. Indoors, under artificial light, the smart gardener should adopt a strategy that works. Many soil amendments and organic fertilizers break down and release their nutrients far too slowly for use indoors. All the plant can use are the ionic form of the elements, and the plant doesn't care whether this is made possible by fungal and microbial metabolism or by chemical refinement. The tricky part lies in supplying all the necessary elements in the proper proportions. This in turn depends upon what is present in the root-zone medium and in the water, as well as environmental conditions (amount of light, heat, humidity, ventilation) and the leaf and genetics of the cannabis strain. (The amount of nitrogen, for example, that would burn the hell out of a Jamaican sativa variety will leave some Dutch hybrids visibly begging for more).

There are many fertilizer brands on the market. The best ones will be found at a garden store

Many successful gardeners use a combination of "organic" methods and mineral-salts on their plants; the art lies in knowing how much is enough, and how much is too much. The best organically-derived fertilizers are those that have already been "digested" by microbial action so that their nutrients are readily available or are derived from mined but unrefined mineral deposit in a soluble form. These include bat and seabird guanos, worm castings, seaweed products and mined deposits such as langbeinite, (Sul-Po -Mag) epsom salts, and greensand. Some amendments, such as chicken manure, blood meal, or fish-based fertilizers should generally be avoided indoors. (They can smell bad and make your plants unhappy, unless you can manage to maintain a truly tropical environment.) I've talked to people who use everything from fish-tank water to worm-bin tea (not to mention rabbit pellets, cricket crap, and iguana guano), but you're on your own there.

Keep in mind that Blackman's Law of Limiting Factors (or the lowest stave law), which informs us that whatever factor is in least supply governs the rate of reactions, applies to our horticultural efforts. This means that applying more of one thing (like fertilizer) will not make your plants grow any faster if something like light levels, root-zone moisture, or ambient CO_2 levels are too low.

Be careful of composted materials, unless you've made absolutely sure that the composting process was thoroughly completed. This is a topic too large to cover here (See *Let it Rot*), but suffice it to say that the presence of insects, weeds and other interesting flora and fauna can be distressing in the indoor garden. We are not trying to set up Biosphere III and replicate the ecology of the Hindu-Kush in our grow-room; the idea is to have a reasonable harvest on a regular basis.

What do plants want?

Yes, energy is matter and vice-versa, but we will concentrate on the seventeen essential elements necessary for plant growth. Cannabis is a weed, and can survive under a wide range of root-zone and aerial-zone conditions, but for your ganja to be *the kind,* the necessary elements and conditions must be provided.

Carbon (C) is the basis of life as we know it, and is supplied safely to plants in the form of carbon dioxide (CO_2), which is present in our atmosphere at a level of 350 parts per million (and rising). Carbon is present in the plant's structural and functional components, as in all organisms, and without its presence growth will cease. Carbon dioxide enrichment may be invaluable in the grow-room if other environmental parameters can be controlled. Combustion generation of CO_2 is appropriate in colder climates and times, but if the heat generated is excessive, bottled-gas enrichment may be employed. This works best if temperature and humidity levels can be tempered with air-conditioning; otherwise, the synchronization of gas-enrichment and ventilation may not prove to be any more productive than constant (flow-through) ventilation. Sophisticated systems for environmental control are available for the technically-oriented gardener, including microprocessor based personal computer programs that will monitor and control everything in your grow-room, including calling you up with an encrypted message when your security system is breached and confirming your flight to Amsterdam. However, that is beyond the scope of this humble treatise. (We're still having enough troubles backing up our hard-drive.)

The next most necessary elements are the atmospheric gases, Hydrogen and Oxygen, which combine to form the ubiquitous and omnipresent compound known as water (H_2O) Hydrogen and Oxygen combine with most other elements in biological processes, and are utilized by plants in myriad metabolic processes which are too complicated to detail here. Suffice it to say, Cannabis requires a moist Root-zone environment, but with enough air-holding capacity to sustain this plant's high oxygen requirements. Fertilizer compounds containing high levels of hydrogenous compounds (such as ammonia) should be used with caution. The employment of oxidized compounds (such as nitrates) will generally prove to be more successful. There are two primary ways to kill plants: under-watering and over-watering. If the root-zone environment of your plants is under-watered to a certain point, the potting medium may develop dry pockets, which lead to wilting, root death, and difficulty in re-wetting. The other extreme is keeping the medium so damp that normal respiration is hindered as a result of a lack of oxygen, and your prized plants turn yellow and die. This overabundance of hydrogen and lack of oxygen can be mistaken for under-fertilization by the novice gardener, with predictably disastrous results; i.e. dead plants. Experience is the most effective teacher.

Now we get to the nitty-gritty of N, P, and K. Nitrogen (N) is present in so many molecular combinations that the actual amount present can be difficult to measure; nevertheless, over-fertilization with nitrogenous compounds is the hallmark of the novice gardener. The wise horticulturist learns to read fertilizer labels and apply the forms of nitrogen that plants can use.

N-Nitrogen Nitrogen gas comprises about 79% of our atmosphere, and there are some organisms, such as Rhizobium bacteria, which form symbiotic relationships with certain plants and "fix" the nitrogen present in the air. Unfortunately, this will do the indoor gardener no good unless rotation planting with beans or clover are planned, as Cannabis forms no such mutually-beneficial relationships with soil microflora. If you look at a fertilizer label, you may become bewildered at the forms of nitrogen available. Organic fertilizers are required to be labeled according to the percentage of soluble and insoluble nitrogen; while mineral-salt based fertilizers will detail the percentages of ammoniacal, nitrate and urea present. The experienced horticulturist is aware that soil and environmental factors dictate the form of nitrogen that will prove most beneficial to any particular plant. Indoors, with artificial illumination, the greatest danger lies in the overuse of ammonia and urea based fertilizers, or of "undigested" organic compounds. Delicate root hairs may be damaged and water uptake disturbed. In addition, the abuse of "hot" forms of nitrogen that are rapidly incorporated by the plant, can lead to soft, weak growth and delayed flowering. A 1:1 percentage of nitrate to ammoniacal nitrogen works well in peat based mixes. In hydroponics the percentage of ammonium compounds should ideally not comprise more that 25% (3:1 ratio) of the total nitrogen present. Nitrate compounds are somewhat delayed in their assimilation by the plant as the oxygen ion is utilized in plant respiration (carbohydrate production). Their judicious use results in a sturdier and hardier plant that is more able to resist pathogens and build up the energy necessary for abundant flower production. (Unless you happen to be growing your cannabis for Cambodian shade-leaf soup, in which case all of the above can be ignored.) Urea compounds may be useful in foliar sprays in the event of a severe nitrogen deficiency but should be avoided in the root-zone. (This is especially true in hydroponics; urea will not register on a dissolved salts tester.) Nitrogen is a mobile element, which means that it can be translocated from old growth to new. A slight deficiency will result in the oldest leaves turning yellow and drying up. As long as new growth maintains its color and vigor, there is no cause for concern. Overdose will be apparent as a browning of the leaf tips; this is a sign that irrigation must be increased, or the soil may even need to be leached of its excess salts.

I thought more fertilizer would make them happy.

P - Phosphorous The elemental form of phosphorous is a lustrous metal which rapidly oxidizes (burns) in the presence of atmospheric oxygen. In biological systems phosphorous serves a crucial role in energy storage and transfer, and is necessary for healthy root and flower development. The indoor gardener should stick to those sources of phosphorous that are readily available to the plant roots. To the "organic" farmer, that means the high phosphorous bat or seabird guano's are to be used in preference to the rock phosphate or bone-meal of the outdoor horticulturist. Refined sources of phosphate salts, such as mono or di-potassium phosphate should be used in hydroponics; slow-release forms such as triple-super-phosphate (a calcium salt) should be avoided. It must be kept in mind that phosphorous uptake by the plant is temperature-dependent. Under cool root-zone conditions, growth slows through the restriction of the energy produced by chlorophyll. This frequently shows up as a reddish-purple hue to the plant as other photosynthetic pigments such as anthocyanins take over the task of supplying energy for the plant. This can be most stressful if the temperature of leaf-zone of the plant is relatively high, as the roots struggles to put up with the demands placed upon them by the leaves. Proper root zone temperature (68-77 degrees F or 19-25 degrees C) thus helps ensure a successful harvest.

While it is true that high-phosphorous fertilizers are to be used during the cannabis flowering cycle, care should be taken to keep phosphorous levels well balanced with adequate amounts of all the necessary elements. Some high-phosphorous fertilizers have a dangerously low pH, which can reduce the availability of some nutrients such as calcium, magnesium and potassium, and even burn plant root-tips. (Hydroponic gardeners frequently use phosphoric acid in order to lower solution pH.) High levels of phosphates can lead to lock-up of calcium and magnesium through the production of insoluble salts, and can compete with the uptake of other anions (such as nitrate and sulfate). Therefore, care should be taken not to overdose your plants on phosphorous in hopes that this will miraculously accelerate flower production, which is in fact dependent on environmental and genetic influences as well as nutrient and water availability.

K - Potassium (The K comes from the Latin word "Kalium", and combined with the Arabic article "al" gives us "alkaline") Potassium originally was produced from the burnt ashes of plants which were placed in large vessels and soaked in water to produce "pot-ash", or lye (potassium hydroxide). Potassium, an integral part of a plant's structure, is also part of an enzyme necessary for the utilization of energy produced by plants, and some biochemical reactions can even take the place of light to a certain extent. This is why crops grown under low-light conditions, such as a winter greenhouse, require more K than those grown in full summer sunlight. A grow room rarely achieves more than 1/4 of the light levels present in the great outdoors; therefore, plants grown under artificial light require correspondingly more potassium that their sisters growing outside.

"Organic" sources of potash include the aforementioned ashes (Hardwood ashes work best; avoid ashes from cardboard because they can contain toxic levels of boron), ground crab or crayfish shell meal, and the favorite, langbeinite, or Sul-po-Mag, which is a mineral that contains sulfates of potassium and magnesium in an available form.

A certain portion of a plant's potassium (K) needs can also be met through the use of seaweed products, both in the root zone and through foliar feeding.

Both wood-ashes and crab-shell meal have an alkaline effect on soil, which must be taken into account. Refined mineral salts that are excellent sources of potassium include potassium nitrate, potassium sulfate, and mono and di-potassium phosphate. Potassium chloride (muriate of potash) is soluble and inexpensive, but should be used sparingly due to its potentially toxic chlorine and sodium levels. The ratio of nitrogen to potassium is important for healthy plant development, and should ideally be at least 1:1.5 in the indoor garden. The nitrogen in fertilizer is listed on labels in its elemental form but potassium is required by law to be listed as K_2O; one must multiply by .83 to obtain elemental levels. Similarly, phosphorous is listed as P_2O_5 and it is necessary to multiply the amount on the label by .44. Fruit development requires even higher levels of potassium, which should be kept in mind if your goal is large amounts of seed production for your pet parakeet.

Other MACRO NUTRIENTS

Ca - Calcium is a major component of the jelly- like filling (cytoplasm) of every plant cell, and works along with potassium in regulating plants' ability to use water. In soils and soilless peat-based mixes, calcium is supplied along with magnesium in the form of dolomite, calcium/magnesium carbonate which also sweetens, (alkalinizes) and buffers the potting mixture. Guanos and some other soil amendments also contain appreciable amounts of calcium. Frequently gypsum (calcium sulfate) is also added. Its effect is negligible on pH, and it supplies calcium as well as sulfur. If the indoor gardener wishes to amend their own mixes with dolomite, care must be taken not to overdo it, as too high a pH will result in chlorotic (yellow) plants due to trace-element unavailability. The savvy gardener who utilizes gypsum should make sure that it comes from mineral deposits and not from recycled wall board, with its binders and additives. (We are all for recycling, but there are a few garden horror stories from gardeners who used wall board gypsum.)

The hydroponic gardener has few choices for soluble calcium salts. Calcium nitrate is the most often used; calcium chloride should be used with caution because of its high chloride levels, which can interface with water uptake. In most hydroponic formulas the calcium-containing part of the mixture is kept separate from phosphates and sulfates, as insoluble salts form if they're combined in a concentrated form. That is also why any one part of a two- or three-part system should be thoroughly mixed into the nutrient solution before the next part is added. Some water contains high enough levels of dissolved calcium that its addition may not be necessary to the nutrient solution; such water may also require the addition of acid (pH-down) to be useful. The best acid to use in situations where the water is very hard is nitric acid, which is also the most difficult to obtain. Most firms that specialize in hydroponics supply phosphoric acid, which is relatively safe to handle, and some carry sulfuric, or battery acid, some grades of which contain high levels of toxic heavy metals.

Mg - Magnesium, the elemental form of which is a light and shiny metal that burns upon exposure to air, is the heart of the chlorophyll molecule, the green energy-producing pigment that bears an amazing structural similarity to the hemoglobin of blood. Plants that lack magnesium develop severe inter-veinal chlorosis on older leaves, which progresses up the plant. Dolomite or hard water can supply magnesium, as can Sul-po-mag or Epsom salts (magnesium sulfate), which has been defined as "organic" in some farm certification protocols. In hydroponics, Epsom salts are commonly used because of their high solubility, low price and purity. Epsom salts can cause "caking" problems in powdered nutrient formulas, because its melting point is lowered when it is mixed with other salts and water held in its molecular structure is released. That is why powdered nutrient mixtures should ideally be refrigerated. Sometimes other salts of magnesium are employed, including magnesium nitrate or magnesium carbonate, but their use can increase costs considerably.

Magnesium is taken up by plants in conjunction with calcium and may be present in a elemental ratio of 1:3 to 1:5 (calcium to magnesium). Low pH levels hinder the absorption of both of these cations, as will low available-oxygen levels.

S -Sulfur is present in all living systems as a component of the amino acids which comprise proteins, and in enzymes such as the vitamins B-1 (thiamin) and biotin. The presence of sulfur is necessary for nitrogen assimilation and the consequential production of chlorophyll; as a result, its lack may be mistaken for a nitrogen deficiency. Found as a soft yellow mineral, elemental sulfur is used in a finely-ground form for acid-loving plants such as blueberries and rhododendrons. Sulfur may also be present in water supplies, and in potting mixes that have been enriched with gypsum. Sul-po-mag and Epsom salts contain soluble "organic" sulfates; hydroponic gardeners generally use a combination of Epsom salts and potassium sulfate. Sulfuric acid used to lower pH and can also contribute to the amount of sulfur present.

Trace Elements are elements which need be present in the magnitude of mere parts-per-million. In some cases their presence in excess can prove to be as problematical to plant growth as their absence. A case in point is boron, the mere mention of which never ceases to conjure up the old tea-heads minds'-eye the image of Ronald Reagan and twenty-mule-teams crossing the Great American Desert. (That was back when corporate-spokesman Reagan was an FBI informant and Democrat. But I digress.)

B - Boron is used by plants to regulate the ratio of uptake of cations and anions, and is of vital importance in plant-cell metabolism. It can be present in appreciable and even excessive amounts in some soils and water-sources, especially in arid regions. Its deficiency can be remedied by ashes from cardboard boxes (about a teaspoon per cubic foot of soil) or borax (sodium tetra-borate; use no more that 1/4 tsp. per cubic foot of soil). In hydroponic solutions borax or boric acid is generally the source of salt.

Fe - Iron is an element that can be present in the root zone on a plant yet remain unavailable for uptake. In soils rich in organic matter, high levels of microbial activity render unusable iron compounds into a soluble form that the plant can absorb. As iron is necessary for the transport of oxygen in plant respiration, its lack quickly leads to interveinal chlorosis on young plant growth. This is most frequently a result of high soil pH. A severe deficiency can be remedied with foliar micro nutrient sprays; toxicity is rarely, if ever encountered. Iron can be provided in "organic" gardens with the addition of a small amount of blood meal or rust (iron oxide)

While older hydroponic formulas may employ ferrous sulfate, iron and the other metallic micro nutrients (manganese, zinc and copper) should be supplied in a chelated form. A chelate (derived from the Greek word for claw) is an organic molecule that holds onto an ion and prevents it form combining with other ions to form insoluble compounds, thereby keeping it available for absorption by the plant.

Mn - Manganese, like iron, is an enzymatic (catalytic) promoter of energy-releasing reactions in plants. An excess of manganese can interfere with iron absorption, and calcium assimilation, but this is not commonly encountered. (Water in some mining regions contains high concentrations of Mn which may need to be removed before it can be used for horticultural purposes.)

Zinc, which is another metallic element that aids plant metabolic processes as a catalyst, and is present in natural auxins (root growth hormones), has a more important function in the regulation of plant growth. Acting as the plants' light sensor, zinc sets the pace for plant growth; the greater the intensity of light, the higher the zinc uptake and the faster the growth. Zinc is commonly used as an anti corrosion for metals (such as water-pipes) and can sometimes be present in toxic quantities, especially in recirculating hydroponic systems with galvanized fittings.

Copper, named for the island of Cyprus, where it was first employed as ancient man rushed headlong into the Bronze Age, is necessary for chlorophyll synthesis in plants. Necessary for the disease-resistance of plants, copper is another element (like zinc) that is occasionally found in toxic amounts because of its use in plumbing.

Chlorine is used by plants in photosynthesis and respiration, but is frequently found in higher amounts than necessary because of the overuse of salts such as potassium chloride, and from the presence of sodium chloride in water supplies. Free chlorine (not the chloride ion) is used as a disinfectant, and may prove damaging to plant roots and beneficial micro-organisms. Therefore, water used in organic-fertilizer regimens should be allowed to gas-off until no chlorine odor is detectable.

Molybdenum is unique among the trace-elements in that it is an anion, and is therefore increases in availability under high pH conditions. Only one Molybdenum (Mo) ion is necessary for a million nitrogen ions, yet it is of vital importance in the assimilation of nitrogen.

Other elements have a beneficial effect in minute amounts, such as nickel and cobalt; and certain elements may not be necessary but can be employed by plants if they are present. This is true for silicon, which can improve pathogen and drought resistance if available in a water-soluble form.

The tricky part of any fertilizer use lies in ensuring that all necessary elements are present within tolerable limits at all times. Observation of your prized "chrysanthemums" is important. The health, vigor, and rate of growth should be assessed, with particular attention paid to the appearance of new growth. (Plants can translocate mobile elements from old growth to new, but the lack of immobile elements can severely stunt plant growth.) And most importantly, MORE IS NOT BETTER: Minor deficiencies and slight imbalances may cause growth to slow; but gross over-fertilization can prove fatal.

Foliar Sprays

Plants can absorb many nutrients through their leaves and stems. Foliar applications of nutrients can help in the case of deficiencies, but are not a replacement for root-zone applications. The most effective sprays are those that supply micro-nutrients and natural plant-growth regulators, such as seaweed-based formulations. This author recommends cessation of spraying after the initiation of florescence (Weird flavors and exotic fungi caused by spraying buds will not make for a happy consumer.) If foliar sprays are used, common sense dictates turning off HID fixtures and fans during spraying, and turning fans (but not lamps) back on until the spray has dried. (Spray droplets can act as miniature magnifying glasses, causing burning.) Research has also shown that the finer the size of the droplets, the more effective the foliar spay will be.

General Hydroponics Flora-series

This nutrient is recommended as a superior plant food. Well fed plants grow faster, provide higher yields and better crop quality.

For the nearest retail location call 1-800-374-9376 or 1-707-824-9376

MaxiGro and MaxiBloom powder formula

EC-TDS
(Electro Conductivity) - (Total Dissolved Salts)

A total-dissolved-salts (TDS) or parts-per-million meter is used to determine the ability of a solution to conduct electricity. Pure water is an insulator; the greater the amount of salts dissolved, the greater the ability of that solution to carry an electrical charge. Technically speaking, conductivity is the reciprocal of resistivity, which is measured in Ohms; so the unit of conductivity is the mho (siemen.) For all practical purposes, 1000 micro-siemens (1 milli-siemen, or 1.0 E.C.) is equivalent to approximately 650 parts-per-million of a fertilizer solution. However, it must be kept in mind that not all salts conduct electricity equally, and a TDS meter will not tell you which salts are present. Nonetheless, assuming all necessary ions are present in the proper proportions, the conductivity will regulate the plant's ability to take up water. The amount of light, as well as temperature, and irrigation frequency also play a role here, because salt levels will rise in the root-zone as water is used by the plant. This is complicated by the increased ability of plants to use mineral salts under higher energy input levels. Simply, this translates into the necessity of keeping a close eye on a garden with high light and heat levels, as salt levels can rise to such a level that plants wilt. Your plants will definitely thank you if you can maintain as little variation in root-zone salt levels as possible. The greatest problems are found in areas with levels of dissolved salts in the raw water supply. This can lead to an excess of unusable ions such as sodium and chloride, or trace-element toxicities.

A dissolved-salts meter.

How to Read a Fertilizer Label 3-12-6

N - expressed as elemental percentages
    Ammoniacal - .7%
    Nitrate......... - 2.3%
    If urea was present its percentage would be listed too.
P - 12% Expressed as P_2O_5 - multiply by .44 for elemental percentage
K -   6% Expressed as K_2O - multiply by .83 for elemental percentage
Ca - 2% of Calcium
Mg - .50% of magnesium
Fe - .10% of iron
Mn - .05% of manganese
Zn - .05% of zinc
Cu - .05% of copper
B   - .02% of boron
Mo - .009% of molybdenum

A fertilizer label that lists the primary sources of the nutrients it contains

    Many fertilizers either do not contain all the necessary elements, or do not list them; these should be used at the gardener's risk.

    In organic fertilizers, nitrogen is listed as to whether it is soluble or insoluble.

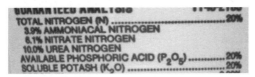

1 pound retail Peters® 20-20-20 before 1996 buyout

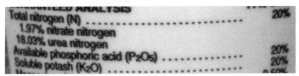

The new Peters® 20-20-20, has changed the source of nitrogen from 10% to 18% urea. This is not recommended for indoor plants.

Chapter 8
Male or Female

How can you determine the sex of your seedlings? Marijuana plants are either male or female, and sometimes both. The female plant is what produces "bud". The role of the male plant is to pollinate the female plant, thereby producing seeds. When you start plants from seed, there is no way to know the sex, unless you flower the plant. Before you shorten the days, you must first take cuttings of each plant, and identify each cutting with its parent. (See chapter 9 for more information on cuttings.)

After a week or two of short days, you will notice the plants showing signs of flowering. The female plants' first signs are the pistils growing directly from the main stem. See the photos for easy identification.

Males will produce fewer psychoactive compounds in their flowers. Unless you are experimenting with breeding, any plant that shows male flowers should be disposed of properly. The cuttings of these males should also be thrown away. One open flower can pollinate and seed an entire room of female plants.

Female flower

Male flower

An example of a hermaphrodite plant

Hermaphroditic or monecious plants have both sexes on the same plant. It is important to keep your eye on your young female plants as they may grow male flowers. This can happen because of stress, genetics or simply from the strong instinct to reproduce in an annual cycle.

This can even happen to cuttings that have grown seed-free, female bud for years. Hormones, or stress, could cause an occasional conversion.

The pistils growing from the main stalk are the first sign of a female plant

Early signs of female flowers

Male plants and flowers

Chapter 9
How to take cuttings

First prepare your rooting supplies, wet the rockwool and mix your rooting hormone if necessary

When you are ready to take the cuttings, remove a branch from the lower half of the plant

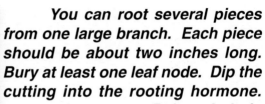

You can root several pieces from one large branch. Each piece should be about two inches long. Bury at least one leaf node. Dip the cutting into the rooting hormone. Poke a hole in the rockwool so you don't bend the stem as you push it in the cube.

Gently surround the stem with rockwool so the cutting does not dry out.

Place under fluorescent lights and your cutting should root within 7 - 10 days.

A flat of cuttings

As soon as roots appear, the plants should be moved into a 4 or 6 inch pot

Step by stem cutting process

Choose your medium, (rockwool, soil etc.) and wet it down. For improved success try water with rooting solution like *Olivias Cloning Solution* or an extremely dilute bloom fertilizer.

1. With a clean, sharp, razor blade, cut at a 45 degree angle. Remove two nodes or leaves below the tip. Remove the lower leaf and adjust the length if need be.

2. Immediately dip the cutting into the rooting solution, (Rootone powder, or a liquid solution). Blow off any excess powder. Only a thin layer is needed. Carefully place into the soil or rockwool without bending the stem. A hole should be made, if one is not already there.

3. Place your pots, or cubes into a nursery flat with a clear dome over the top, and put directly under two or more fluorescent tubes. The increase in humidity will support the leaves from drying out until the roots develop.

4. Monitor your plants closely for the next seven days. Problems or success can happen quickly. Remove the lid at least once a day to allow fresh air to enter the dome, or place a pencil under the corner of the lid to increase the air flow. Keep a close eye on the watering needs. You want the soil or rockwool moist, but never soaking. Air flow is helpful for the plants, but the humidity must stay high until roots appear on the underside of the soil or cube.

5. Ideal soil and air temperature is 74 degrees.

6. Always take more cuttings than you need in case you have some failures.

Fluorescent light promotes rapid rooting. You can continue growing them under these lights for as long as you like.

Use a clear dome to increase the humidity. Transplant the cuttings into soil as soon as the roots show.

Note: Too much humidity can promote the growth of pathogenic fungi and bacteria. It is important to have good air circulation. A pencil under one corner will allow air flow inside the dome.

The obvious advantage of taking cuttings is that a superior plant can be kept alive indefinitely through its cloned offspring. This concept has been effectively applied to agriculture and horticulture for centuries. All *name* variety plants are propagated by the clone method. Another distinct advantage of cultivating a group of identical plants is that you are able to experiment with every other aspect of the growing situation. You may try out different fertilizers, amount of light, soil mixtures, etc., on some of the plants while using another group of plants as the control. You can be sure that the differences in the plants are due to your experiments and not to inherent differences in the plants themselves. This is especially valuable to the grower who wants to experiment with the crossing of marijuana varieties.

You should be able to predict, with the careful observation of the parent plants, the growth rate of your clones, their susceptibility to certain diseases, their reaction to fertilizers and their projected date of flowering.

After the new plants start growing in their four inch pots, let them grow under fluorescent lights until you are ready to flower them under your HID light. This process will allow you to develop a continuous cycle without timely delays. Or for larger plants, grow the plants under a halide until they are half the size of your final desired size. Then cut the light down to 12 hours. Remember, the plants will keep growing for a couple weeks after you shorten the daylight.

This plant had cuttings taken from the lower half of the plant

Rooting hormone is recommended

Early stages of a female flowering plant, about five weeks from harvest

Chapter 10
THC Chemistry

It is not the intent to delve deeply into organic chemistry in this book, however, a basic understanding of how marijuana attains its "stony" qualities is useful to the grower for breeding and growing techniques.

The resins of marijuana are manufactured by tiny glands on the surface of the plant, not in the roots. These glands come in a variety of shapes and are most prominent on the flower tops of female plants. The tops will become coated with an almost crystalline covering of resin. The amount and chemical composition of the resin determines the potential of the plant to affect the smoker.

It is uncertain what use the heavy resin production of cannabis serves in nature. It may be that the sticky resin deters insects and mites which reach their heaviest populations in late summer and early fall, the same time that the plants go into their heaviest resin production. It may also help the flower heads resist fungus and mildew, also very active in the fall. It is assumed that the resins protect the leaves from drying out and from burning by the sun. Whatever the functions of the resin on the plant, there is no doubt about its effects on humans. The psychoactive effects can be traced to three main active ingredients: THC (tetrahydrocannabinol), CBD (Cannabidiol), and CBN (cannabinol). Of these, THC is by far the most important. In a refined state, THC is definitely a hallucinogen, ranking with LSD, mescaline, and psilocybin. While it is clearly impossible to grow plants that are pure THC, the goal is to grow them with as high a THC content as possible.

THC does not appear all at once, ready made in the plant. THC, like other complex molecules, is synthesized from other compounds which the plant derives from the soil. The building of compounds by the plant is called biosynthesis. Plants are chemical factories, building complex components from simple ones, after first manufacturing the simple building blocks used. The plant must first produce CBD before it can produce THC.

CBD, by itself, has little or no effect on humans. Combined with THC, it changes the quality of the "high" obtained from marijuana. If there is a large amount of CBD, combined with THC, the effects are often described as "sleepy" or "stupefying". Headaches and loss of coordination seem to be associated with marijuana containing large amounts of CBD.

When THC breaks down, CBN is the by product. CBN is mentally active by itself but far less potent (about 1/10) than THC. High temperatures over prolonged periods are conducive to the conversion of THC to CBN, so it is wise to store marijuana in a cool place. High temperatures do not have that effect on marijuana that is still growing, unless the flowering tops are left on the plant too long and become "overripe".

In the early stages of growth, the plant is usually less potent than in later stages. The CBD production levels must be heavy in early growth so that THC can be biosynthesized by the plant in later life. The breakdown of THC to CBN should proceed slowly after harvest so that the potency does not break down along with the THC. Choosing seeds from marijuana with the desired effects will result in a crop of plants possessing the same characteristics. Drying and curing the final product in the right way will help to retard the breakdown of THC.

Information available to the public is limited since governmental research does not usually deal with how to grow more potent marijuana, and private research is prohibited by law. Fortunately, the common men and women in hundreds of countries have done much of our research for us over a period of thousands of years.

A THC molecule

The THC, CBD, and CBN molecules are very similar in structure

These "crystals" of resin on the flower tops are a pretty sight

This indoor plant is undisturbed by harsh rain, wind and other possible elements.

Outdoors the plants are subjected to the weather

This marijuana top appears to be Cannabis sativa.
Notice the thin leaves

Chapter 11
Pruning & Pinching

One of the difficulties novice gardeners face is the proper way of bending and shaping their plants to conform to the space at hand. This can become especially interesting when different strains with different growth habits, are grown in the same space. The aim is to utilize the emission characteristics of the H.I.D. lamp in such a way that the flowering tops of your plants receive the maximum light possible, without removing the leaves which are doing the work of photosynthesis. "Pinching" the growing points of the plants in order to encourage branching is generally begun after the appearance of the fourth set of leaves. This results in a plant with two growing points which may be further pinched into four or more flowering points. Other techniques, such as horizontal trellising, wires and weights for bending, and vine-clips to hold up flowering tops may be necessary when your plants threaten to overwhelm the space allotted to them. (Ideally, you have planned for the inevitability of all your heavy-budded plants falling over.) Remember, any part of a plant that is not receiving proper levels of light or ventilation can become a breeding ground for pathogenic micro-organisms.

In a room with a low ceiling, you may have to bend the stem. Do this by gently pinching the stem. The top will fall over, and grow to the side.

90

Prior to Harvest

As harvest time approaches there are a couple of things you can do to increase the resin production and improve taste.

This cola will be ripe in about two weeks

As the buds are near finished, some leaves will turn yellow

These plants became so heavy that stakes were necessary to hold them up. Thanks to archaic laws the colas, or buds, are worth their weight in gold.

When the tops are ripe

Harvesting the flower cluster at the right time is very important. You want to pick them when the "colas" have gained the maximum weight, potency and fragrance. Precise time will depend upon your genetics, and environmental conditions; careful observation and experience are required. Remember, the buds will be reduced by as much as 85% in weight once they have been dried.

You do not want over or under ripe buds. The premature buds are smaller and the overripe buds have lost some THC due to its conversion or breakdown into CBN. Indoors, the tops can remain on the plant a little longer than they can outside. The climate is milder, and you will not suffer losses through violent storms or freak weather. The metal halides produce less ultra violet light than found outdoors which seems to be a

factor in the degredation of the plant after it has completed its life cycle.

To determine the point in time when most of the tops are ripe, you can keep an eye on the hair-like filaments coming out of the colas. These hairs will be white in the early stages of the blossom. New white hairs continue to grow, increasing the size of the bud.

At the same time the bracts holding the empty seed pods will begin to swell with THC. You will notice an i n t e n s e fragrance, a spicy aroma, and the resin-filled buds will become sticky to the touch.

At some point, usually 8-10 weeks after the short days began, most of the white hairs have ceased growth and turned red. At this point and time you need to harvest. It may be a day or two late. You will learn the best time with experience.

Other indicators of maturity.

You may notice small peaks of flower clusters, or a "conehead" effect that indicates that the bud is finished ripening.

The number of leaves on each cluster. You have no doubt noticed the progression of leaves on a beginning seedling from one serrated leaf, to three leaves, to five etc. There is a similar occurrence on a maturing bud, in reverse.

Once you have determined that the tops are ripe, you are ready to harvest. Harvesting should be done in the heat of the day, i.e., plan your harvest so that the lights will have been on for 12 hours.

This very large bud is a result of extremely high light levels and the plant's genetics.

This plant was grown under a metal halide light.

Harvesting & Drying

This drying room is equipped with an exhaust fan and circulation fan. The larger colas are hung, while the smaller tops are layered on screens. To insure even drying on the screen, the buds should be turned every couple of days.

Drying your plant must be done properly; the moisture level and the taste depend on it.

The best method is to cut the plant at the base of the stem and hang the entire plant upside down for several days. Drying time will vary depending on the temperature, humidity and air circulation. A dark area with lots of air flow, between 60 and 70 degrees, is ideal. The humidity should be medium, about 40%. After the buds seem to have absorbed any available resins from the leaves and stem, (about 6-9 days), trim off the largest leaves and groom the plants. Continue to circulate the air and to rotate the bud to keep it drying evenly.

After a couple more days it is extremely important to check your buds frequently. Although they may take as many as 12 to 14 days to dry, it is important to follow the drying process so you don't over or under do it.

Don't bag up your buds too early. Make sure the bud is completely dry. If you bag it up too early it will spoil the sweet taste. Mold can quickly take over and spoil the crop. Mold can also be very harmful if inhaled, especially for people who may have immune deficiencies or lung problems.

Other drying techniques:

Brown paper bag. After hanging your plants for about a week, groom the plant and categorize your leaf, from the buds, and place a single layer of buds in a grocery sack. Occasionally shake the bag, turning the buds. The paper bag method allows even drying.

Hang'em - Keep the plants on the stem until they are crispy dry, then groom and bag.

Light it - Test the product. When it burns well it might be done.

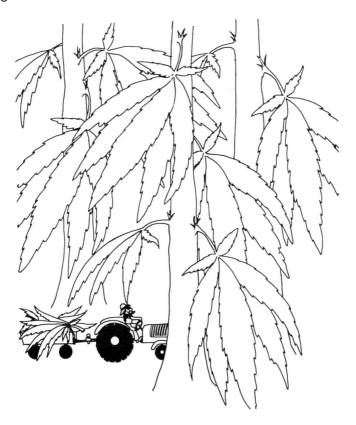

Buds hanging to dry, and on a screen to allow air flow

Keys to drying

Good air circulation and ventilation.
Humidity not too high.
Avoid direct sun or bright light.

The drying room

*Hanging the plant seems to be the best way to dry
your buds evenly*

After trimming your plants you can scrape the resin off your fingers and roll it up: "home made hashish"

It is important to keep your area clean. A clean garden will reduce problems such as pests, disease and mildew.

Chapter 15
Insects

The praying mantis is one of the most well known predator insects. One of these can keep your garden free of pests, and they make good pets too.

Marijuana is a vigorous plant. It grows wild in most of the tropic and temperate zones of the earth. It is, nevertheless, heir to some of the vegetative pests and diseases that infest other plants.

The most common infestation that strikes marijuana is the spider mite. They are not easily spotted in the preliminary stages of infestation and by the time they are really noticeable, they will have already become firmly entrenched. The first signs of the spider mite infestation are pinprick holes on the under side of the lower leaves. They seem to attack the mature leaves first and then quickly spread upwards as the colony increases in population. The mite itself is a yellowish color and can be seen easily with a magnifying lens or with a good eye. Soon after the spots appear, tiny delicate webs form. The mites will be crawling slowly on or near the webs. The spots and the mites themselves are very small and by the time you can plainly see webs, you have a full fledged infestation on your hands. The multiplication rate of this minute arachnid is truly prodigious. Left to themselves,

they will soon colonize every available leaf, sucking them dry of vital juices. Red spider mites, the most common mite found outdoors, are seldom a problem in indoor cultivation. However, they can

be introduced to the plant from the outdoors on the fur of pets or can be carried in on other plants. Prevention is key. If you do not allow the introduction of diseases or insect pests to your growing room, you

will never have to deal with them. Summer is the most likely time for spider mites to infest. During this time it is teeming with microscopic and insect life. A simple walk through the garden may result in your picking up an unwanted

Mites living on a bamboo stake

passenger on your sleeve or shoe and depositing them right in the middle of the most desirable growth environment possible, your healthy plant. Early detection is the key to avoiding serious problems with mites. Temperature control and humidity levels are also very important.

Spider mites are the most common pest problem but certainly not the only problem. Aphids, whitefly, thrips, and fungus gnats are other potential pests. All of these bugs, including mites, can be easily eliminated if you take steps to prevent them.

Early detection is crucial if you want get rid of them in short time. You do not want your bud threatened by an army of bugs.

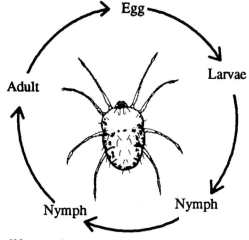

Egg

Larvae

Adult

Nymph   Nymph

Spider Mite life cycle
- Development usually occurs on underside of leaves.
- Eggs hatch in 4-7 days.
- Immature development time: 7-14 days.
- Spider Mite produces 50-200 eggs.

The spider mite life cycle will increase with higher temperatures.

Pyrethrin is an organic pesticide that will kill adult mites when sprayed directly on the bug. When treating spider mites with pyrethrin you must spray every five days, for three weeks.

Classic signs of spider mite infestation

Once the webbing appears, you have a difficult battle ahead

Pesticide

Because you may consume or inhale your plants in the near future, organic pesticides are a must. No one wants to use chemical pesticides on their plants. Unfortunately you sometimes need a fast effective cure to rid your crop of bugs.

Be aware that organic pesticides will likely break down very quickly, so applications need to be repeated.

Insecticidal soap is the safest possible bug killing product you should spray on your plants. It breaks down in a matter of hours, and is not at all effective on mites unless you wash and wipe every leaf, a difficult chore.

Pyrethrin is a common ingredient in many vegetable sprays. This product will break down in 24 hours outside, but it may last as long as 10 days in a lower light condition. This is possibly the most commonly used pesticide on vegetables. It should kill most pests on contact, but they keep coming back. Continue to work on it, be consistent, change products occasionally to reduce the possiblity of the bugs building up a resistance to the product.

There are many products on the market, all of which will do harm to the bugs, the plants, and you. Read and follow the labeled instructions, and do not use a product unless it is approved for use on edible plants.

Fungus Gnats are another common pest that you might encounter. This little gnats' larvae eat the organic matter in the soil. They will eventually disturb the roots. The recommended treatment is a biological larvaecide called Bacillus Thuringiensis serotype H-14 (BT), sold under the label of "Knock Out Gnats" or "Gnatrol" made by Abbott Laboratories. Make sure that the BT is specific for fungus gnats.

Thrips are another common insect that will invade the foliage. They leave small snail like tracks in the leaf. They will not destroy your garden but they will cause problems and setbacks. Blue sticky traps are the recommended organic method.

Beneficial Insect Control

Another way to control pests whithout any pesticides is called integrated pest management. This involves the use of predator insects that eat the pest or use the pest as host for their own eggs. This ultimately kills the pest and allows the predators to breed.

This practice is effective, but it is not as easy as you might hope. Unfortunately, the bugs are costly and sometimes the bad bugs breed faster than the good bugs.

There are many predator insects on the market.

See the chart on page 123 for assistance in selecting the correct predator insect.

There is Fungus Among Us

Fungi will attack plants at any stage. Lack of air circulation is the leading cause of fungus. It can infect stems, leaves, soil or flowers. Some susceptible strains will be more likely than others to obtain molds, especially when the plant has experienced stress or drought.

It is advised that you simply make certain you have adaquate circulation and ventilation to prevent fungus from settling. Watering too soon, spraying too much or misting

flowering plants are likely times you will experience fungus.

The first problem with fungus may arise with the cuttings. Keeping a dome over the starts is very helpful for rooting, but without enough air circulation you may get mold on the tips of the leaves. In this case you need to remove the dome, and cut off the leaf to prevent the continuation of the mold.

When you are drying your plants you must not bag your buds too soon. Not only will this ruin the taste, but it may be harmful for someone with lung problems.

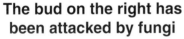

The bud on the right has been attacked by fungi

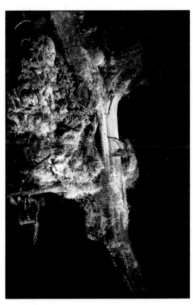

Chapter 16

Hydroponics

There is no one right way to cultivate cannabis, but there are techniques and methods that can greatly increase yield and quality within the confined spaces where this weed is forced to grow. Chief among these is the automated feeding and watering system called hydroponics, which includes all necessary mineral elements in a soilless rooting medium, ultimately providing a gourmet smorgasbord for your prized plants.

Hydroponics is derived from Greek words meaning "the working of water." While there is archaeological evidence for horticultural methods that employed nutrient solutions and inert media, such as the Chinampes of pre-Colombian Mexico and the hanging gardens of Babylon, hydroponics as we know it grew out of scientific research into plant physiology that culminated in Professor W.S. Gericke's public demonstration of fourteen-foot tall tomato plants at U.S.C. in 1938. While it has provided salads to air-bases and submarine crews', and is extensively employed throughout the world on a commercial basis where available soil and water are scarce, hydroponics has (perhaps deservedly) become a buzz-word among US law enforcement authorities whose calling it is to make inmates out of gardeners. So be careful what you say, and to whom: but with a little knowledge, most of the necessary parts and fittings may be purchased at any hardware store. The proper nutrients may be a little more difficult to procure without resorting to mail-order or a trip to the nearest large city.

The major difference between soil and soilless gardening is that in hydroponics the roots of the plants are contained within a non-nutritive (inert) material, and all essential elements are provided in a liquid form. In some advanced systems, there is no medium at all and the roots just hang in a misting chamber (aeroponics) or in a thin layer of solution (nutrient flow technique, or NFT), however, these methods are more prone to failure and are not recommended for the novice gardener. A properly designed home hydro unit will provide the toker or baker with a year-round stash without the back breaking labor of hauling large sacks of soil, and therefore is especially appealing to the apartment-dwelling or physically disabled gardener.

Soil and many soilless potting mixtures have a great ability to "hang-on" to nutrients and gradually release them over time, a property known as "buffering" or "cation-exchange capacity" (C.E.C.). Some of the necessary plant nutrients are positively charged, and are known as cations. These include calcium, magnesium, ammonium, potassium and molybdenum. Negatively charged essential ions or anions are always provided to the plant in solution form, regardless of what type of garden one grows; these include phosphorous sulfur, nitrate, and the metallic trace elements. Mixes that include peat moss, clay or large amounts of organic material such as sawdust, cow manure, compost or bark will behave much differently than inert hydroponic media will.

General Hydroponics
"Power Grower"®

115

These media differ in their electro chemical properties of repulsion and attraction, dictating the type of fertilizer used, as potting mix with a high C.E.C. may already contain or be enriched with necessary nutrient, and are therefore prone to over fertilization. This author has seen cannabis grown hydroponically in everything from broken bricks to ground-up tires, but the most commonly used substrates are horticultural rockwool and expended-clay aggregates, followed by perlite, pumice and other volcanic lavas, pea gravel, vermiculite and various combinations of whatever is available. Materials to avoid are those that react unfavorably with the fertilizer solution, and these include limestone gravel, metallic slags, insulation-grade rockwool, mortar (while usually broken bricks work just fine) sawdust, and builders-grade sand. An ideal medium will hold an adequate amount of water and air while providing support for the plant. "Adequate" is determined by the intervals between irrigation, and the type of irrigation employed, and is further complicated by such factors as heat, humidity, ventilation and leaf area.

Which hydro unit is best for you?

The hydroponic system that will work best for you is determined by how large an area your garden occupies and by your level of technical expertise. The simplest hydro units, such as wick systems supplemented by regular hand watering, will work as well as a soil-based garden and will allow the gardener the luxury of an occasional vacation. The increase in productivity engendered by active, timer-controlled irrigation systems also requires an increased attention to details including solution pH, conductivity, and temperature. However, the intrepid gardener with half a lick of common sense can become a successful hydroponic horticulturist as long as the needs of the plant are understood and provided for.

WaterFarm® by "General Hydroponics" is easy, reliable and a favorite for beginners. Retails for about $50.

WaterFarm® is compatible with the Controller Systems. 1 to 12 units can be interconnected.

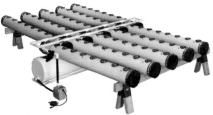

AeroFlo® is an exceptional system for growing large numbers of small plants.

The philosophy of the covert closet cultivator who turns to hydroponics should be K.I.S.S. (Keep it simple, stupid!). There is no need to reinvent the wheel. Stick to tried and true methods, at least until you know what you're doing. Complicated plumbing connections should be simplified and made as leak-free and accessible (in case of possible failure) as possible. As you progress up the learning curve, you can change and experiment with more advanced techniques; but beware, because the closer to the edge you venture, the more fraught with peril is the trail. A well-designed system will keep your plants alive even if there's a power or pump failure, and not require constant minute-to-minute attention.

The materials used in the construction of hydroponic gardens should be non-corrosive and non-phytotoxic. Most plastics can be used for containers, tubing and fittings as long as they are rated as safe for potable water and food handling applications. (Look for the N.S.F.-National Sanitation Foundation approval). Copper, brass, aluminum, steel, and galvanized materials should be avoided, but stainless steel, fiberglass, enameled and plastic coated surfaces are usually serviceable. A major imperative is the avoidance and containment of leaks and spills. (Unless you want to explain to your landlord the peculiar plight of the endangered Chaco Canyon cave fish that inhabit your closet every time your hydroponic reservoir starts dripping through the ceiling of the apartment below.)

A wick system

Passive hydroponic systems like this one will afford convenience but will not provide optimum growing conditions.

118

Water pH - The acid/alkaline level of the water should be between 6 and 6.5. Test the water with the nutrient added, and adjust the solution with pH Up or pH Down.

PPM - Parts per million, is an indicator of the level of nutrients in the water. Marijuana plants can tolerate up to 2000 PPM. 1000 PPM is recommended under average conditions. PPM or T.D.S. meters do not register urea nitrogen, so be sure you use a quality hydroponic nutrient that is free of urea nitrogen.

There are many different ways to apply hydroponics. This toilet system was functional.

These healthy plants are growing in rockwool. The tub floods and drains four times a day.

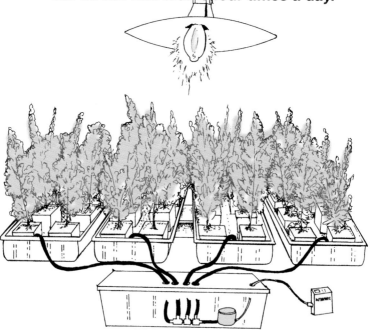

Ebb & flow system

When the pump turns on, the bed is flooded. When the irrigation cycle is completed the solution returns to the reservoir via gravity.

120

The heater is in a glass pyrex pan. If the reservoir was ever empty the heater would not break.

Air is pumped through the air stone keeping the water oxygenated. This is very important.

Troubleshooting

My HID light is not working.

First be sure your lamp is screwed in tight.
Look at the capacitor, if it is bulging it is bad.
Confirm the lamp is functional by testing it in a different ballast.
HPS - Have the starter or ignitor checked.
Be sure you are burning the proper wattage bulb and ballast. The ballast is dedicated to that wattage.

My leaves are discolored.

This could be a wide variety of problems, but most likely is a pH imbalance, your soil is too acidic, or you have spider mites. It is also possible you are using an inferior fertilizer.

My light is on a 12 hour on/off cycle and the plants are not blooming.

The plants must get complete darkness during the night hours. Any light will keep the plants in a vegetative state.

Fresh air is very important for a healthy garden

Pest	Description	Treatment	Predator
Spider Mite	Very small spiders that discolor the leaf, webs will form when infestation gets worse. The most common insect pest to attack the indoor garden.	Treat repeatedly with organic pesticide such as pyrethrins or soaps. Apply at least every 5 days for over 3 weeks.	Beneficial Spider mites 50-100 mites per plant every 10 days will control the mite population.
Aphid	Pear shaped soft bodied insects that come in many colors, usually green. Easy to see on the new growth.	Aphids are easy to kill with a soap solution or pyrethrin. Repeat applications every 5 days until they are gone.	Green lacewing, Lady bugs, or Aphid parasites.
Fungus Gnat	Fruit fly sized, soil dwelling pest that doesn't cause harm to the plant, but they are a nuisance. The larvea may disturb the roots.	Most any pesticide will kill the adults, but you need to kill the larvea in the soil. Gnatrol or Knock out Gnats is a biological larveacide.	Beneficial Nematodes. Recommended for rockwool.
Thrip	Often in the soil this pest will leave slug like tracers on your leaf. Usually attacking the lower foliage.	Blue sticky traps laying flat, or pesticide such as pyrethrin. Repeat frequently, and during the dark cycle.	Thrip predatory mites, thrip parasite, green lacewings, or pirate bugs.
White Fly	Very difficult to kill, easy to see. They lay eggs that hatch and suck the sap from the leaf.	While pyrethrin will not work you may have to try Bio-Neem, or something stronger in order to eradicate this pest. Diazinon is a very nasty pesticide that may work. Just hope you don't get white fly.	White fly parasite (Encarsia formosa) Whitefly Predators (Delphastus pusillus)
Scale	Brown, round shell covers the adult usually located on the stems or under the leaf on the veins.	To get rid of these pests, the best thing to do is wipe them off with a cotton swab dipped in rubbing alcohol. Then rinse with warm water. Tedious, but effective.	Scale predator
Mealy Bug	Similar to the scale with a cotton like appearance. Gathers around the stem and leaf.	Do the same thing you would do to get rid of scale. Both mealy and scale are not likely to reach your garden unless you mix other plants with them.	Cryptolaemus Beatle or Green Lacewing

Leave enough room to get around, otherwise watering will be difficult. In small closet gardens it is helpful to use a watering can that has a long neck.

Don't shock your plant. It will stunt the growth.

This hanging plant had to be weighted down in order to keep it from growing into the light.

Chapter 18
Security

Security is of paramount importance to the outlaw horticulturist. There are an amazing number of law enforcement agencies and authorities who have make the search for manufacturers of schedule **1** substances such as cannabis a high priority. Until the laws are changed, and the War on Drugs is over, the guerilla gardener must be discreet and proceed on a need-to-know basis. Growers should learn to keep all written and electronic correspondence about their illegal activities to a minimum, and not say anything to anyone about their interesting hobby unless it is absolutely necessary. The propaganda poster from World War II that reminds us that "Loose Lips Sink Ships" springs to mind; most growers serving prison sentences are there because they said the wrong thing to the wrong person. Frequently, people who are arrested on drug charges are offered lighter sentences in exchange for information which leads to other arrests. Advertisements are run in various media outlets that exhort the populace to "Turn in a marijuana grower" and tell them what to look for. Disaffected "friends" and former lovers can be potential sources of grief; and to make life more interesting many law enforcement agencies employ undercover officers and confidential informants, who have made it their business to find out what your business is.

In the past, strategies devised to ferret out felonies of the botanical kind have included the setting up of "sting" operations, such as the establishment of phony gardening-supply firms; legitimate companies, especially those whose advertisements have appeared in "counter-culture" magazines have had their shipping records seized and their customers busted. Federal agents historically have a record of infiltrating political organizations, so be doubly careful if your interests tend toward activism. (Yes, you should be paranoid; they are watching, and they are out to get you.) Orwellian, Gestapo - like tactics designed to enable closet cultivators of cannabis are even targeted at children the most vulnerable segment of society. Education campaigns such as D.A.R.E. where in turning in your parents is encouraged as a patriotic act, are just one example of the effect the War on Drugs (read the "War on Human Rights") has had on a society in which "euphoria" is classified as an adverse drug reaction.

In all other dealings the prudent gardener should proceed with common sense. Loud and wild parties and heavy traffic at all hours of the day and night should be avoided. Ostentatious displays of wealth can only serve to alienate those neighbors who equate wealth with success.